The FISH in the TREE

A play by Julia Donaldson

Illustrated by Andy Elkerton

Characters

Jill

Jenny

Bill

Lenny

Kenny

Penny

3

Bill enters, carrying a box, a fish and a cheese.

Bill: Hello! I'm Bill. Maybe you're wondering why I've got this box and this fish and this cheese? Well, I found the box under the floorboards. And do you know what's in it? Oh dear, here's Jill – I'll have to tell you later.

Bill hides the box, fish and cheese. Jill enters.

Jill: Hello! I'm Bill's wife, Jill. I **must** tell you something. Bill's got terribly smelly feet!

Bill: Jill just can't keep a secret. She told the whole village about my smelly feet.

5

Jill: No, I only told Jenny.

Jenny, Kenny, Lenny and Penny enter.

Jenny: And I told Kenny.

Kenny: And I told Lenny.

Lenny: And I told Penny in the shop.

Penny: And I told all my customers.

Bill: And soon everyone in the village was teasing me.

Kenny: Is that fish I can smell?

Jenny: Or is it cheese?

Lenny: Or maybe it's cheesy fish – or fishy cheese?

Penny: No, it's just Bill's feet!

Jenny, Kenny, Lenny and Penny exit, laughing.

Jill: Don't forget we're going fishing, Bill.

Bill: Okay. Fetch the net and we'll go.

Jill exits.

Bill: I was going to tell you what's inside my box, wasn't I? Well, it's full of gold coins! But if I tell Jill she'll tell everyone, and then I bet someone will steal the gold. So I've made a plan. See this fish? I'm going to hide it in a tree.

Bill hides the fish in the tree.
Jill enters with a net.

Jill: Let's go to the fish pond.

Bill: No, let's try fishing in this tree.

Jill: Are you mad?

Bill: No. Can you reach that branch with the net?

Jill lifts the net up.

Jill: Well I never! I've caught a huge fish!
Just wait till I tell Jenny.
Jenny! Jenny!

Jenny enters.

Jenny: What is it, Jill?

Jill: Look what I just caught!

Jenny: What a gigantic fish! Was it in the pond?

Jill: No, it was in a tree! Let's go and fry it, Bill.

Jill and Bill exit.

Jenny: Kenny! Lenny!

Kenny and Lenny enter.

Kenny: What is it, Jenny?

Lenny: Yes, what's going on?

Jenny: Jill says she caught a fish – in a tree!

Kenny: Poor old Jill. She can't be very well.

Lenny: Wait till I tell Penny in the shop. Penny! Penny!

Penny enters.

Penny: What is it?

13

Lenny: Jill told Jenny she caught a fish in a tree!

Penny: That's ridiculous! Wait till I tell my customers!

Jenny, Lenny, Kenny and Penny exit.
Bill enters.

Bill: That was part one of my plan.
Now for part two!
I'll drop this cheese in the pond.

Bill drops the cheese in the pond.
Jill enters with the net.

Jill: Let's see if we can catch any more fish in the tree.

Bill: No, let's try the pond this time.

Jill: All right.

She dips the net in.

Bill: What have you caught?

Jill: Well I never! It's a huge cheese!
I must tell Jenny.
Jenny! Jenny!

Jenny enters.

Jenny: What is it, Jill?

Jill: Look what I just caught in the pond! An enormous cheese!

Jenny: Are you feeling all right?

Jill: Yes, I'm fine. Let's go home and eat the cheese, Bill.

Jill and Bill exit.

Jenny: Kenny! Lenny!

Kenny and Lenny enter.

Lenny: What is it, Jenny?

Jenny: Jill says she caught a cheese in the pond!

Kenny: Oh dear. She must be joking, mustn't she?

Jenny: Let's tell Penny.

Lenny: Penny! Penny!

Penny enters.

Penny: Well? What has Jill been saying now?

Kenny: She says she caught a cheese in the pond.

Jenny: Poor old Jill. Do you think she's ill?

Penny: No. I think she just enjoys telling silly stories.

Jenny, Lenny, Kenny and Penny exit.
Bill enters.

Bill: Now it's safe to tell Jill about the gold.

Bill picks up the box. Jill enters.

Jill: What have you got there, Bill?

Bill: It's a box of gold coins. I found it under the floorboards.

Jill: That's amazing! We're rich at last!
Wait till I tell Jenny.
Jenny! Jenny!

Jenny enters.

Jenny: What is it now, Jill?

Jill: Bill has found a box of gold coins under the floorboards.

Jenny: Why don't you go and lie down, Jill?

Jill: No, I think I'll go shopping! Come on, Bill.

Shops

Jill and Bill exit. Kenny, Lenny and Penny enter.

Kenny: What's Jill been telling you now?

Jenny: Something about a box of coins under the floorboards.

Lenny: Not another of her silly stories!

Penny: Yes, I don't think I'll bother to tell my customers.

Jenny, Kenny, Lenny and Penny exit. Bill enters.

Bill: Well, I think that's done the trick. The gold coins are safe!